From Splintered Soul

Scott McBride

FriesenPress

Suite 300 - 990 Fort St
Victoria, BC, V8V 3K2
Canada

www.friesenpress.com

ISBN
978-1-5255-6613-4 (Hardcover)
978-1-5255-6614-1 (Paperback)
978-1-5255-6615-8 (eBook)

1. POETRY, SUBJECTS & THEMES, DEATH, GRIEF, LOSS

Distributed to the trade by The Ingram Book Company

To my Dad, my incredible kids, the many wonderful mental health caregivers, my courageous colleagues in Group, and to all my loving, supportive family and friends who gave me hugs and hope when I needed it most. Thank you for helping me walk back into the light once again!

TABLE OF CONTENTS

▍ STRUGGLE   31

▌ REDEMPTION   81

PREFACE

Mental illness plays no favourites; neither does pain, guilt, sorrow, nor succumbing to that deep wailing cry of desperate surrender that remains unheard, within the white noise of our existence. Every hour the cliché of 'Misery loves company' gets validated, and yet, we rarely ever hear each other. Consequently, our hurt intensifies because of isolation, sometimes self-imposed. Other times we're just ostracized from a world that doesn't understand or has no patience to try to comprehend us. But misery *does* need company.

Sharing my poetry was unexpected. All of it originated from some bursting floodgate of darkness and awareness too, but it was a private, fiery venting on paper, never even to be read again. Then group therapy happened, and I was immersed in an ensemble of the bravest people I have ever met. We all shared in the pain and frailty of being human. All of us understood the craving to stay curled up in bed and not engage in the day, and the only reason we might rise at all was because our collective bladders demanded it! So within this special gathering, I found my 'company', and the poetry became my journey's language, my voice.

I am also extremely blessed to have an incredible, loving and supportive sister, Laura. She is my kindred spirit and my inspiration to begin exploring (very, very slowly mind you) the many realms outside myself. She is the one who saw value and purpose in my writing, and thus began this adventure to publish poetry, quite the shift from teaching finance. None of this would have happened without her efforts and encourage-ment. Yet, it all began with one very anxious step: to share the misery of a Splintered Soul. Welcome to my company!

Scott McBride - July 2019

DESCENT INTO DESPAIR

Free-fall, I plummet

Ground rising to christen Doom's

Voyage of sorrow

SAND'S DEMISE

A blistering, white-hot branding iron
Has scarred my world
Leaving a frozen tundra
Of lifeless, scorched nerves
With the blackened numbness
Of a frostbitten mind
Where actual feeling, true sensation
Is a threat to the pulse
Which somehow lingers in the monotony
Of barren hopes

Deep shadows coalesce
In the chill winds of a desert night
Biting, coarse, unimpeded
The barrage pummels
The flesh of sanity raw
A crimson legacy for the sand
The sentinel surrenders
Into the embrace of the dune
The abrasive bed
A silicate tomb
To eyes final glimpse
Of violet skies
Pierced by the silhouette
Of my own smiling face
Still grasping the glowing iron

POPPY LEGACY

The poppy stem twists and undulates
Like its alkaloid offspring's impact on the brain
Morphine! Codeine!
Pristine bliss from a red petal's gift
So rise from Flanders
And the escape we shall harvest
To dull the war of the modern frontline
The infiltration, like slow decay
Decomposing resilience
Until numbness
Renders one to ignorant oblivion

WOLF SHADOWS

The shadows are ravenous
Emboldened by my weakness
They encroach en masse
A swath of dark wolves
Bringing an angry midnight
And a hunger unsated

The flailing attempt to escape
Ignites the coordinated
Pounce on the prey
The juice of despair
Drips from their fangs
A pulsing blackness
Fades to final surrender

THE OPEN WOUND

The severed vein to my well-being
The hemorrhaging in my soul
Spurts daily mayhem
Requiring the direct pressure
Of mindless routine
Still the leakage will not scab
A cut artery of a hemophiliac
With tension-wraps turned scarlet
The wound never closing
The spirit ever weakening
The light-headedness of too much loss
Brings dimming awareness
With the dark anaesthesia
Freezing out reality
Leaving only the null and void

REAPER'S KISS

Tantalizing
Impatient with anticipation
Wanting for so long
Thinking for hours each night
The rush, the thrill, the need
Tender at first
Like a flutter on the corners of your lips
Then the fullness of flesh
Compressed in heated softness
And then, the pull on your mouth
To open, to succumb
To the probing passion of Death's tongue
Swim in the sweet euphoria
Of bliss nocturnal
As saliva's shared
The poison's placed
The weak knees of desire
Become the collapsed pulseless body
Where survivors despair
For the one who fell for the Reaper's Kiss

CHOKE OF LIFE

The cloak of despair
Wrapped like a tourniquet
Restricting any trickle of hope
Dribbling through the veins
Of this lost spirit
As the surrender to sadness took hold
And the sips turned to gulps
Of the emboldening vodka
With a culminating chaser
Of tiny pills to make one happy
The final descent began
To the oasis of quiet
To peace
To nothing
Yet something unexpected
Transpired between
Mouth and throat
A Choke of Life
Which spewed the dark momentum
From this moment of despair
While the black numbness remained
So did the pulse
So did the writer
Of the Choke of Life

REMAINING STILL

First engulfed in loss, then just lost
Immersed in the hell of the hurt
The totality of the cost
The relinquishment to assert
Any strength beyond the comatose will
To exist by remaining still

Stagnant objects swept up alone
Sorrow's tornado be the cause
Like Dorothy twisted from home
Dizzied with the new world of Oz
Where murky paths that shadows fill
Now frozen and remaining still

Trepidation, now the guide
A cautious banner waving fear
The white flag surrenders and hides
Dark spectres encroach ever near
Circling their trapped quarry until
The prey bolts from remaining still

Escape but fleeting in the gasp
Of movement's freedom in the run
Breathe fully the sweet air you grasp
For this breath shall be the last one
And once your lungs completely fill
Hope's exhaled while remaining still

▍ LOST IN THE CHANGE

Rooted in the stupor of the past
I clung to its vapor trail
Of false promises
Always on sale
As I breathed so fully
In a space so confined
Truth of the moment
Was left far behind

A rudderless journey
With no return trip
One can spin in the currents
Of a directionless ship
Yet even climbing to the vantage
Of the crow's nest spire
No ports are calling
To replenish Hope's fire

I am lost in the change
I needed to make
To just rearrange
And not fear mistake
I am lost in the change
Of being better than now
As if being the sage
Was fruitless somehow

Ah, the wisdom of the sage
One ready with a cure
Expressed in a riddle
With answers unsure
The golden panacea
Remains forever concealed
Until we own our own struggle
And certain truths are revealed

Like you being better
May mean being alone
When the impact of the past
Has crushed the solace of your home
The break is harsh
The cut is keen
The goal, yet far
Though hope is seen

I am lost in the change
I needed to make
To just rearrange
And not fear mistake
I am lost in the change
Of being better than now
As if being the sage
Was fruitless somehow

▌ FROM SPLINTERED SOUL

A compound fracture mends
With time and numerous pins and screws
Yet a fractured spirit does hope end
For what does one have to lose
A corroding heart disappears
Rusted by reality's toll
The cloak of dread draws ever near
To smother my splintered soul

Immobilized by a rotting will
Barricades to joy like Mordor's walls
Stands stalwart over the deepest hole
The silence of the dark hangs heavy and still
As one last breath before The Reaper's call
I surrender my splintered soul

WHEN HAIKU

When do the tears stop?
When will curling up in bed
Not define my day?

ACCELERANT HAIKU

The accelerant
Was the alcohol fueling
Depression's embers

TREATMENT HAIKU

I need some treatment?
Like water-proofing my brain
From rusting despair?

SAD GRUDGE HAIKU

I carry a grudge
With anger and sadness mixed
Of tomorrows lost

HEAVY HAIKU

Mediocrity
Is a Life of sweet blessings
Once risen from Hell

CRINGING CRY

My heart throbs so blue
Each cringing beat cries for you
Tears' wall must pass through

IN

Into the Empty
Inurned in the black vacuum
Inside sorrow's soul

LOST (PART I)

Looking aimlessly for purpose
Observing what lies ahead with fear
Suffocated by worry and the past
Trembling at the unknowns of tomorrow

THE VOICE

I've been here before
The seduction of finality
The raising of the knife
The emptying of the bottle
The calling of the pills
The Voice is louder now though
Cognizant of the failure
To break my grasp on life's pulse
The first time around
The dark spectre is learning
It is keeping pace
With any forward motion I can muster
The shadow tranquilizes
Any thought of consequence
I am just logging-off
"You need to shut down."
The soothing Voice reminds me
The echoes caressing my soul
Like a nourishing mantra
A blank haze overtakes me
As I enter the taxi
I don't remember calling
On my way to the hospital
Time disappears
My eyes fixate on the light switch
As one arm gets manipulated
Into a blood-pressure cuff

I'm assisted off the gurney
A dopey trance registering nothing
But the coolness of the breeze
Assaulting the open back of my hospital gown
A dark uniform on either side
Support and escort me
Down blaringly bright hallways
Security? . . . Needed for me?
Ah yes! No risk to others
But to myself ?
I'm handed off at the nurses' station
Signatures go on forms
Like a UPS special delivery
I have succeeded
My numbness saved me
Like a reflex of self-defense
Which quiets the horrors
For but seconds
Enough time, this time
To move beyond the range
Of the Voice

GRIEF YET UN-GRIEVED

Mere days past did cherished soul leave
    Insides churning, present steps stumbling
With the grief yet un-grieved
In a year from now will I cry my plea
    To assuage the burning, to quiet the rumbling
Of a broken soul's insanity

Saturated love blessed days, years . . . each second past
    Such mighty heights, so high to fall
Now soaring dove leaves tears to last
With sorrow's hold growing strong and fast
    The healing light, its meager crawl
Gets dimmer in tomorrow's dark cast

Within the shroud without reprieve
    All the yearning, so fruitless in voice
Echo in the abyss of silent screams
And hinder hopes of future dreams
    Locked tightly in, without choice
From the grief yet un-grieved

▌ THERE'S NO FURTHER DOWN

No further down
Swallow hard the heavy loss
A poison pill of pain
Descend below Hades with heavy cost
No thought of ascending again

Swim in the vitriol of despair
The searing oil burning out hope
A desperate inhale of toxic air
As aching limbs thrash in the moat

There's no further down
I've climbed to the crest of the bottom
There's no further down
All joys are forgotten
In the foundation of the black
Souls adorn a midnight gown
And within the waltz of Shadows' attack
One can dance no further down
To the precipice one spins
As the Host of Darkness leads
Your honoured soul, a relished win
No matter your frantic need
You sense this Tango's final cries
The crescendo crushing solid ground
Yet from this place you can only rise
For there is no further down

▌ INDIFFERENCE

My world has paused
Not with pain or anger
But in speechless disbelief
That a reflex of caring
Derelict in its duty
Deserted its post
During a crisis of despair
Heartless imposed pragmatism
Distanced the need, awareness or desire
To triage hemorrhaging sorrow
Instead pre-meditated abandonment
Like a cleaver
Severing support and hope
Alone . . . bandages of feeble resilience
Leak loneliness until senses go black
The eyes roll white
The body folds over
The mind grasps
The final realization of betrayal
That one who was expected to love
Chose the opposite road
During a partner's greatest need
Indifference

▌ HANG ON

As I scream out loud
And clench my fists
This angry cloud
A choking mist
I fear to see
Reflection true
What's become of me
What shall I do

Hang on
All I can do is . . .
Hang on
Even when all hope gone
All I can do is just . . .
Hang on

The curtains drawn
My skies are black
No brightening dawn
At horizon's crack
I want to flee
What I can't subdue
What will become of me
What can I do
Out the door
Just one step
Courage asks more
Than what's given yet

One stride to free
What's long overdue
What will become of me
What shall I do

The stomach's rise
To my throat
Clouded eyes
Too remote
With certainty
Doubt holds true
What will become of me
What shall I do

Hang on
All I can do is . . .
Hang on
Even when all hope gone
All I can do is just . . .
Hang on

▌ QUICKSAND OF REALITY

I put on a brave face
I put on a false face
Jovial, engaged but vacuous
Empty of the substance
The moments deserved
I am better than this
Yet even playing pretend
Is a struggle
As the dark
Quicksand of Reality
Embraces me in a straight-jacket
Of relentless descent
Perhaps just the simple effort
Of dawning rose-coloured glasses
Will materialize a sufficient lifeline
That within my flailing motions of dismay
Fingers will grasp
A tether of promise
Now it is just a matter
Of whether I have the strength
To pull myself out

WHAT'S THE POINT?!

Angels gaze from heavenly perch
A self-luminescent throne
Radiating eddies of warmth
Into the ether

Well . . . that's about as helpful
As trying to get tan
From Uranus
I don't live in the ether either
There might be a little bit of methane *ether* hanging around
At ground level though
Especially, after a lonely plate of deluxe nachos
And the six . . . I'm getting even lonelier beers
At least I get numb-drunk from the beers
And every 20 minutes
I know my kidneys work
The angels aren't even there to hand you
Another roll of butt wipe when you need it

Where are these diaphanous spirits
Of goodwill and compassion?
Good people, kind people
Their giving souls decomposing
As their endurance to despair
Breaks beyond healing
Perhaps these useless ghosts of benevolence
Could serve a practical purpose
And become co-conspirators

In a raucous night of liquid escape
"Hey Clarence. Shake those bells again
Cause we're gonna sing
One bourbon, one scotch and one beer!
You're my true buddy now!"

THE MOMENT

The moment hung there
Like the witch's glossy apple
Buffed to brilliance with dark agenda
Awareness yet spoke in silent wisdom
A cautious note
To a necessary risk
Where footing would be lost
Sliding down the scree of uncertainty
With no perch to grasp
The moment hung there
Knowing it would be embraced
By one with no choice
But who must tread onward
Unbalanced, unsure and into the unknown

▌ I YET

I observe the obvious
Yet still neglect the necessary
I understand the need
Yet can find no satiation
I can feel an expanding grin
Yet shrivel at any thought of hope
I understand the struggle
Yet the battle never ceases
I look towards the setting sky
Yet know the sun may not rise

BRAIN WORMS

The intertwining, coiling
Worms of my brain
File their blunt heads
Against the abrasive
Inside surface of my skull
Trying to hone a fine dagger
To finally
Get the point across
To my addled awareness

It is drugged in delusion
Novocaine feeding the soul
Exist without existing
Waiting for the taser
To either shock one into coma
Or to bolt awaken with eyes
Defibrillated to witness
A different horizon

The landscape is flowing,...
Morphing with what-ifs
From tantalizing to despair
Life within the current of extremes
Agony and bliss
Just two sides of the coin of existence
And existing is a moving target
Where you are the bulls-eye
And the archer

The challenge is
The act of living
Where the proverbial ducks
Are never in a row
But have taken flight
To everywhere

ANNIVERSARY

Anniversaries
Celebrations?
D-day, Hiroshima, 9/11
All horrors
But worth remembering
August 2nd, 2018
A life almost taken
By the one
Who almost lost it
Remembering is automatic
The horror still palpable
The celebration?
I'm here for the anniversary

STRUGGLE

Flailing while sinking

One treads to capture a breath

Of life in quicksand

STARTING BLOCKS

In the starting blocks
Muscles ready to explode
Away from the past
Thrusting forward
With the fury of fear
Of looking back
Bang! Bang!
Fuck! False start again!

Takes forever
Just to get prepared
For that moment
When you create
The breeze of your own freedom
Now bent over again
Locked into the position
Ass in the air
Vulnerable to reality's ramming
When the blocks
Remain the shackles of a status quo
Unforgiving in its demands

Fingers on the line
"On your mark . . ."
Legs coiled, hips raised
"Get set . . ."
Wait for it!
BANG!

Just one Bang!
Run dammit! Run!
Don't look back!
Faster! Keep going!
It's your race now!
And the starting blocks have become
Invisible

THE GRIP ON REALITY

I am beginning to find myself
While remaining lost
As if existing
With untold unknowns
Is a prerequisite
For this achievement

It forces the building of callouses
To withstand reality's rope burn
The grip unrelinquished
Even with slippage
Well-being sustained
By still holding on

▎THE PULSE OF HURT

There is a benefit
To emotional self-flagellation
Your heart still beats
The whip strikes
To the groin of the soul
Keeling over in agony
While invigorating the pulse
Meting out reassurance
Through scars of awakening
That pain compresses
The heart to beat
Until another shaky breath
Inhales at the coiling
Of the next strike

BEYOND THE SHACKLES OF PROPER

I feel a teenage lust to rebel
Against all that is proper
To embody a Trumpian disregard
For cherished mores
Of compliance
And soar without
Pragmatic shackles
That parasitic leech of an existence
Sustained by necessity and responsibility
I want to excise
This mundane status quo
With Mr. Hyde's
Phoenix of hunger
Subdued only by the absence
Of carnage to others
But let the juice of passion remain
Dripping along each moment
Like a succulent wine
To be savoured in the rush
Of its sensory glory

▍TOO MUCH FEEL

There is a higher gradient
To being sentient
When one is overwhelmed
With the essence of what that means
To *feel:*
Agony intensifies the senses
Light . . . burns
Touch . . . assaults
Hearing . . . thunders
Smell . . . chokes
Taste . . . poisons
Senses become the abyss
Resilience the breaking dam
Future?
The fine line between
Treading and drowning

▎ DEPARTURE OF THE GREEN

It's funny (dark 'haha')
How the removal of 20 or so plants
Back to their original owner
Feels like a plasma drip
Clinging to the past
With the valve now closing

Initially, I cared for the plants
For her
But after a year of tending
Their well-being was for me
They're gone now though
With the furniture
With the commotion
And with the giggles of my son

The plants gave me oxygen
To care for something
When caring for myself
Felt like cursing
The weeds in the garden
Disgust! What's the point?!

Now, I miss my plants
And how they grounded me
In routine and sustenance
For my well-being

Perhaps this is why

Struggle

I bought flowers this week
Just for me
3 bunches for $20
Purple, pink and white
Sitting pretty
Keeping me company
After the departure of the green

KEEP KICKING

Brave is swimming across
The toxic, turbulent river of hurt
The current playing
"Monkey-in-the-Middle"
With your resilience
Tossing you about:
The proverbial ragdoll
Flung again and again
Against the embedded rocks of reality

Submerged without bearing
Scrambling for the next breath
As you somersault your way
To the panicked intake of oxygen
To fuel your next stroke
And the inches of progress
Barely discernable
To the other side

One thought guides your will
"Just keep kicking!
Damn it! Just keep kicking!"

THE BLANK STRUGGLE

I am drawing a blank
An empty canvas
Coated corner to corner
With myriad shades
Of invisible

I am gnawing a mirage
An empty stomach
Craving sustenance
Within a vacuum
Of nothing

I am pawing at pretend
An empty grasp
Clutching wind
Within the void
Of blindness

BREATH IN THE WIND

Each day begins
Competing with the wind
Bleached world spins
Deleting giddy grins

Dawn's phony break
Only billowing greys matter
Pawns left to forsake
Lonely prey for the Mad Hatter

Gusts of reality
Gnaw at the true
Lusts for finality
Saw through sinew

Lonely the harsh breath
Trust-clogging doubt
Homely effort at best
Must keep fighting this bout

Second attempt
To deeply inhale
Reckons my contempt
To not harbour the 'fail'

▎ SURRENDER

I shall surrender to the unknown
And embrace my anxious existence
Along the ledge outside my home
Where living includes some resistance

My sofa's lure has steadily grown
Hooking my backside with persistence
Pillows dented as my comfort zone
Now released by renewed insistence

To rise and give my legs a chance
To tread the dirt and leap the mounds
To acknowledge there is no decree
But to take part in the dance
Where life's rhythm and pulse are found
My surrender can now set me free

MY DOMAIN

The silence echoes
In ripples of loneliness
Rebounding off the drywall
With deafening clarity
Waves of confirmation
That the space is truly empty
40 watts of yellow
Make a feeble attempt at welcome
More a suggestion of jaundice
Inflicted upon the air
Sickly, Withered, Hopeless
This is my domain
This is where I inhale
The toxins of sadness

Yet, this is also where I reign
I choose
Succumb to the decay
Of a scurvied soul
Or bear down hard
On the window's rusted lever
Cracking free from the
Stagnancy of dread
And permitting the eddies of possibility
To fill my lungs
With the sweetness of wonder
Where each exhale
Is but anticipation for the next breath

This is MY domain
Let the echoes be
From a vibrant heart
Pounding permission
To let the breeze in

TRUTH, TIME AND PAIN

This may be the moment
To honour the pain
And just let the torrent
Of anguish leave me lame
Sorrow's spell is now sent
Casting shadow in life's frame
With darkness now a resident
In playing grievous game

The hurt becomes a cleansing fire
Where the soil of joy is charred
Yet this ash is where new hope must dine
And from meek roots stems rise higher
From soul's drought they shall be barred
And nurtured by waters of truth and time

▋ THE UNSURE JOURNEY OF SUBSTANCE

"What one can not handle, give to God"
Yet the handoff of hurt without faith
Admits to the Divine as a wraith
Gives false pretense to prayer's solemn nod

Still, should this gesture of need feel odd
When seeking Heaven without a face
Perhaps in the search one leaves a trace
Where the Spirit's welcome can be caught

The genuine journey answers not
Beguiling questions unanswered still
No matter how potently we yearn
Our own truth lies beyond what is sought
During the travels of our free will
We find the guidance from which to learn

COMPASS

Magnetic North shoots so straight
Frenetic course always late
Poetic remorse models fate
Inside hides my compass

Gravity sends to the ground
Cavities rend any hope found
Levity ends with no sound
Inside hides my compass

Enough dark already shows
Rough and stark is how it goes
Tough with bark for tomorrows
Inside hides my compass

▍ LOST – PART 2

Looking through shadow to mist
Observing small steps forward
Suffering only the crystal ball
Trembling at just standing still

WHAT CAN POSSIBLY DESCRIBE?

Get out the thesaurus
I'm in need
Of a word
A phrase
An adjective
A descriptor of the indescribable
Some dose of diction
That conveys crisis and healing
All crashing with confused chaos
But like a scalpel
Cutting through the noise
To simplify the complex
Into a singular nugget of wisdom
That sweeps in the messiness of the past
Like raking leaves after an autumn storm
That draws in the challenge and courage of the present
Like the pull of the tides against the sands
That envelops the circling 'what-ifs' of the future
Like hovering vultures sensing wounded prey
Or like the swirling winds
Stirring the adventurous possibilities of a 3-masted ship
Where can I find the literary equivalent
Of a Theory of Relativity
For the moving target of my depression

Yet while the pendulum of depression
Sways from mild melancholy to silencing despair
The essence of me remains constant

Struggle

Aha!
That's it!
The eureka phrase to encompass it all
I am here

▌SHADOW'S GUIDE

The shadows lurk
But they are always behind you
Each step is your own
As it falls into the light YOU create
Any shaded path
Has cast its shroud
Independent of the one
Entering this dark forest
Yet sometimes
We are without bearing
And may find ourselves
Lost wandering along
Clouded paths with egg-shell footing
Still terra ferma
Only with sharper edges
Pricking us with the clarity
That we have a pulse
A drive. A need
To move forward
Even without
A finite destination
Even with pain
Mixed with the promise
Of each stride forward
Where you will always be
The shadow's guide

FOG WISDOM

The fog's mist is cool on my cheeks
The moon's glimmer diffused
Within the diamonds of moisture
A suspended vale of translucent night
Shading paths from direct intent
Leaves stumbling feet
To veer in ignorance
With only the unforeseen collision
Alerting me to a journey
Now without bearing
Rising scarred and bloodied
My altercation with camouflaged obstacles
Has enlivened me through hurt
It pounds with stubborn defiance
"I am ALIVE! Notice ME!", it cries out
The mist still eddies about my boots
The view . . . a dull cataract-inflicted grey
The challenges ahead, plentiful
Daunting and very likely pain-inducing
Yet within the fog's mist
With the coolness on my cheeks
I feel that pulse to rise again

THE BIRD HAS FLOWN

I teeter on the crest and break
With a granite cushion down below
No softer landing from this heartache
But she will never know

To the winds she's flown
With wings strong and sure
Her nest with me she's outgrown
And no cage can she endure

Freed from monotonous skies
Life's flourish will take hold
Her future will not have to answer Why's
Only her passion and drive to be bold

My nest now has too much space
As I shrink with being alone
No courage there to replace
The loneliness of this home
Yet while I stay in one place
My own joy I can bring
As sweet breezes filled with grace
I shall open my mouth and sing

▌ HURT

Oh my god this hurts
And I just had to watch
Reruns of 'Glee' to rub it in
She will be gone
My son will be gone
It is necessary for all of us

It brings the sort of pain
That discombobulates the senses
Numbness is not possible
Tears are inevitable and endless

Caring will now be accomplished
Like a course on-line
Available and connected
But with geography and reality
Minimizing those efforts
To a failing grade

My mental illness played a role
Instability could not be weathered
When others needed
The security of sameness and routine
Yet there's a natural re-balancing
Into a new equilibrium
Where the flow of futures
Find equal potential
In the serene pond of normalcy

FACE SONNET

The character of a man lies in his face
The crinkly lines etched about his eyes
Become deeper still when smiles arise
And fills the room with warmth and grace
The noble nose has a dignified place
Confirming the visage both humble and wise
A wicked grin beckons mischievous ties
And echoes of laughter resound in the space

This wrinkled face remains so aware
Attuned to the whispers of sad souls
Needing that melting embrace to ease woes
A thoughtful patience listens with care
Then my Dad's soothing voice fills the air
With all the love he can bestow

▐ TINGLING STAR

Sweet memories serve the needed hope
When I've lost such precious jewel
The treasure of your smile a safety rope
Pulling me to renewal

My loss is Heaven's gain
For the Universe now can share
The brightest soul in midnight's pane
An eternal vigil of an angel's care

When you walked the earthly sand
My heart drummed sweet content
With guiding love you took my hand
And a million steps we spent

I wander a little lost for now
Yet my fingers recall the feel
Of a father's grasp that could endow
The wonder of dreams made real
Whether starry sentinel or tingling palm
I sense your presence still
Through pain of loss or tranquil calm
My days you will always fill

COMMANDO OF SANITY

Shelter but a moment
In the wink of two glimpses
Through cloudy gauze
Destination alights
For camouflage shadows not
In the starless night
Where dark is dark
Like a cave ground under
A muddied eclipse
Descended beneath horizon's push
Denied glimmer's birth
Yet night extinguishes
Naught but light
The might of blind steps
Guides through faith
Not felt in bones
Foreign to hope
Yet remains a path
Hidden, sparse, dangerous
A Commando's precipice
Of decision
Move on or reside
On the edge of the abyss
Inertia of purpose
Finds motion taken
Departing the descent
But unknowns now entered

Explorer's resolve
A vigilante's boldness
Stirs courage unwarranted
As forward pull
Like a magnet's fury
Draws the scope in tightly
Where in the wink of two glimpses
Daylight breaks

AUTHENTIC HAIKU

Facades broken down
By the harshness of the hurt
Just the real remains

THE PROCESS HURT HAIKU

Such bureaucracy
Applying for LTD
Made to feel ashamed

NOT QUITE A SUCCESS HAIKU

Made my bed today
'Happy days are here again!'
I'll add sheets next time

SUPPOSED TO BE SAD HAIKU

Today I felt guilt
At spontaneous laughter
I've no right to joy

▌CHAIN ENVY HAIKU

Dear Ebenezer
My chain is bigger than yours
Sincerely, The Reaper

▎ YOU THE AUTHOR

Pages past haunt the present
Like a murderous rampage
With no clues to acquiesce
The nervous twitch
To scan for the moving spectres
Lurking behind you

Every few steps
More deeply ensnared
Within the web of dread
Like the next helpless victim
Caught in the cruel plot
Too late for Sherlock Holmes
To have deduced your fate

Yet who is the creator of your story
Who drafts the wonder
In those pages unwritten
Who . . . by stepping forward
Who . . . by inhaling the breeze
Of unknown tomorrows
Creates their own plot twists

You live the adventure
Of your own existence
Pathos, Passion, Glory, Pain, Exultation!
All manifest through you
Just breathe, explore, create and engage
As the Author
Of your Book of Life

OUTSIDE THE BULL'S-EYE

Consider the bull's-eye of a dart board
That is my comfort zone
That tiny circular prize
Is now a home base
For my well-being
Yet my being well
Necessitates movement
Outside this self-imposed sanctuary
Into the score of possibilities
That will strain the calm
That will stir the stress
But that will also,...accumulate more points
To my healing

I yet feel the weight
Of the Darts of Life
In my own hand
The courageous throw
Aims at the randomness
Of the board
Not the hub of the wheel
More value is earned
With forays to the perimeter
A broader boundary
For testing limits
And erasing limitations which
Fear, reluctance and worry
Can so corrosively, yet subtly inflict

On a player's fragile stance
But that IS the issue

Fragility
The vulnerability at existing outside this
Tiny womb of safety
The bull's-eye is curling up in bed
With little urgency to rise
Comforted by the nothingness of each hour
Accepting of the numbness
That so restrains the joy of the spirit
Which adventures uncharted could bestow
To the uncertainty and risk
The Board of Life represents
It is time for the uncoordinated left-hand
To fling the Dart of Possibility wildly
Into the 'what-ifs' beyond the centre
Where fragility is expected
As a part of the human condition
And the randomness of the dart's destination
Sets the stage for living
Outside the bull's-eye

▌ MUSINGS

When did rising from bed become a decathlon event?

Every time I hear that motivational ballad "Rise Up", it always leads to phallical depression!

What does the future look like? Depends™, Dentures and Death!

▌ *THINGS TO IMPROVE ON* HAIKU

Assertive mantra
Live without your two kneecaps
Or get me my drink

▌DESSERTS BACKWARDS IS STRESSED

The good days tease me
Like the second chocolate almond
Wanting more
But reaching into an empty bowl
When the sun rises again

When one endures for so long
The Dessert of Life: Joy
That sweet carb of happiness
Is withdrawn from the diet
Of one already shrinking with depression

This depleted menu
Leaves me fasting on fear
Harvested in my own
Garden of blight
Where seeds of sorrow flourish

There's always a plentiful crop
Of dark sustenance
And should a shortbread of hope
Take an esophageal ride
Bulimic thrust resumes the acidic norm

The body rebels against laughter
Fun, friendship and love
And stagnates into
A cirrhosis of the soul
And a life dark and tasteless

There is only one remedy:
Walk to the nearest Dairy Queen
Order a hot fudge sundae
And plunge your entire face
Into that sticky, glorious ice cream bliss

IN MIND'S EYE

In a Mind's Eye
Dwells thoughts unspoken
Dreams untouched
Daring un-risked

In a Heart's Sigh
Remains which are broken
Leave pain as the crutch
To a forgotten kiss

In a Soul's Cry
Tears become tokens
Of a toll asking too much
To retrieve what's lost in the mist

RING OF CONFIDENCE?

Confidence brings pain
When formed of paper mâché;
A welter-weight sparring
In REALITY'S heavyweight ring?
"And in this corner
We have Scrawny Boy
Trying to wear Big Boy shorts
Tooooooo BIG!"
Better off wearing
Depends™ with sparkling stripes
Much better fit
And superior protection
For when your desperate exertions
Yield more substance
Than just profuse sweat

Thus prepared
Staying in the ring for a few rounds
May just add some plaster
To that light-weight shell
Hardening up the jaw
For that upper cut
You couldn't dodge
Time for some Rope-A-Dope

▌ A FOGGY TOMORROW

Tomorrow wobbles on the edge
With the dark abyss salivating
In anticipation
For this eroding stance
But a temporary perch
From dire descent

For now, words cement the ledge
As if writing is a mason formulating
His creation
To solidify the chance
That a sudden lurch
Is not imminent

In this there is no certainty pledge
That Murphy's playful manipulating
And misdirection
Is mere happenchance
To obscure the search
For what is meant

HOPE IN SHADOW

My role as husband
As father, as teacher
Has been amputated
From my daily *raison d'etre*
As if to create a vacuum
Pour ma raison d'esperer
Defining who I am
My core values
My purpose, my fulfillment
No longer knotted vicariously
To the vibrant energies of others
This isolation plays two-faced
A withdrawal into the sublime silence
Of loneliness
And the opportunity to choose
Is this my freedom?
Was *choice* not available before?
Or just the lack of assertiveness to make it happen?
Yah! That would be it!
Living in the wake of those
Who blaze their own trail
I'm stunted like the tiny sapling
Stretching for the nourishment of the sun
While much older and larger siblings
Eat the plate clean
No crumbs
The withered die

Returning to the earth
Yet in time there is regrowth
With deeper roots
Brought on by the lesson of the struggle
Sufficient sustenance
Feeds through to new life
Fiercely grounded
Its famished fibres always aching
For the more which is never there
Yet branches yearn higher
Within cover of shadow

SPINNING EVOLUTION

Swirling darkness dizzyingly revolves
Around once radiant spirit which now dissolves
The spinning recedes as day-therapy falls
And an inner clarity slowly evolves
Still so many questions remain unresolved
Just 'stay in the moment' and future answers will be called

▌TEETER-TOTTER

Teeter-tottering:
An abrupt form of ebb and flow
Using thrust from one side of a board
Balancing on a metal fulcrum
In order to defy gravity on the other side while laughing!
Now examine the consequence of mass
Suddenly departing the board at its resting point close to earth . . .
What happens?
A crash landing of the elevated mass
On the other side
Reality and gravity the end culprits
Of play turned nasty, no laughing

Depression is to sink and leave a mark
From one's rapid descent
Being the lone high-rider on the teeter-totter
Before the weight of joy and stability
Slip off the other end of your life board
And your smile gets broken
Your hope smashed into a dust cloud
Of lost particles of your soul
You fall off the teeter-totter
Concussed and unsure
Slow to rise and very, very reticent
To find your seat on the board again

▌ IN THE MOMENT

"Live in the moment"
That's the constant advisory refrain
So one does not become
Drawn and quartered
By the chaotic rush of worry
Threatening to trample us
What if the 'moment' is SHIT though?!
Anger, frustration
A seething powder keg of emotions
And a fuse brightly lit
And an ever expanding tremor
Foreboding the final
SHATTER!
Like a tornado obliterating the surface
With a scar miles long
It is just pure destruction
When forces overwhelm
Living in the moment

▌ STILL BREATHING

The hurt of still breathing
Stirs memories around
It's better than bleeding
Eroding underground
The trials are not fleeting
Resolutely they pound
An awareness so needing
For life barely found

GRIEF AND THE RE-BUILD

I am not what I was
Only now can I acknowledge
That no negative label
Is leeching onto my daily efforts
Of rebuilding and renewal

Yet, I must grieve the lost me
There is pain here
Part of me is measured by the past:
The focus, the drive, the control . . .
The openness to spontaneity and fun

Curiously, it is the 'fun'
I most want to recapture
As if silliness and laughter
Are the main dishes
For my fulfillment

To dance in a thunderstorm
To sing proudly off key
To laugh so hard
Your belly cramps as you cry
And ugly stuff streams from your nose

These are the giddy moments
Of delicious living
Like the decadent cake icing
Which risks premature consumption
While still on the spoon --- Mmmmm!

But as the architect of my new world
I am first grounded in foundation-building
The structure of resilience
Built with blocks of courage
Hewn from quarries of hurt

These walls are unexciting
And painfully slow to erect
Somehow, the 'lost' part of me
Is stirred into the mortar
Not forgotten, but adding strength

I am now a construction site
Of possibility
A work never to be completed
But content in the excitement
The next renovation will bring

REDEMPTION

A Flower may be overwhelmed

by the storm but still blooms the next day

▎MUNDANE JOY

Our stress-fed tunnel vision
Preempts huge blocks of awareness
As if the stage curtain is
Prematurely closing on the production
Any minuscule remainder
Of our mindfulness
Remains smothered in myopic malaise!

Curiously this brings us an upside
To the challenge of mental illness:
It is in the act of *trying* to heal
Where our sensory dullness
Fades like fog before noon
And elicits a higher order
Of observation onto the simple
Versus trying to grapple
The tireless beast of depression into submission

There is a realization that each inhale
Has a smell:
Lilac in spring, wet slate after a thunderstorm,
Petroleum in the traffic jam with the windows down
That each gaze has a unique lens
That shade of green within the grass
Changing with each aisle of mowing
The forest path in autumn
Carpeted with amber, rust, saffron and crispy brown
Adding a little crunch to the colour

Beneath your boots

Even if stepping beyond the threshold of the front door
Proves to be an obstacle too daunting
There remain interior insights:
The lightness of the suds
While washing the pots,
The *ka-chunk* sound of the fridge compressor
Kicking in to join the resonant thrum
Of the dishwasher changing gears
The coarseness of old coffee grinds on your fingers
As they're dumped into the compost bin
While also triggering the craving for beans
Freshly ground the next morning
There is that addictive warmth
To remain under the blankets
But eventually drawn into the daily tug-of-war
With the invigorating option of a pulsing shower,
A scrub brush and tea tree oil soap
All of which spark the jump-start
For the continued rise of you and the sun
With momentum assured
Hopefully accompanied by clean clothes,
Groomed hair and brushed teeth
The mirror is now entitled to grin with pride
At the reflection it is able to bestow

The routine of our lives
Is sweet with the essence of our spirit
Its very simplicity grounds us

In the beauty of unique repetition
Once open to the experience

As the day closes with final rituals:
A prayer, a diary entry,
Enjoying a favourite author's last release
Or even creating some verse of your own
Notice the level of quiet rise
As you slide your attention
To the evening's habit
Caressing you with peace and effortless calm
As you get lost in
Another precious moment of the mundane

OH!

Oh! Divine Sand!
Let your golden warmth
Squeeze between my toes
In an abrasive caress of contentment

Oh! Crashing Waves!
Pierce me with your liquid symphony
Rising to crescendo
To the time of Nature's baton

Oh! Glorious Sun!
Burn out the scourge that besets me
Leaving me exorcised but whole
Within the blanket of your sanctifying beams

Oh! Thunderstorm!
May your rumbling majesty
Ignite a crescendo of life
Cleansed of doubt and regret

Oh! Universe!
Please make space for me
In your wondrous vastness
For I am part of you

▌ MISSIONARY

Missionary
I am in an uncharted jungle
Rich with wonders and dangers
Yet I search for the purpose
Which burrows deep in the mud
Where my feet tread

I quest for me
No! For what is beyond me
Outside myself lies true meaning
Inside myself lies reason
But the current in my Amazon
Rests uneasy in the pool of status quo
Ignorant of the wonders
To be explored and feared

Yet this home base of normalcy
Vanishes with each stride into the forest
The journey, the adventure
The unpredictability
Is the Missionary's bliss
Of emboldened faith
Fueled by unanswered prayers

PLAYING BY NEW RULES

The game has changed
And so have I
The piece I play
Still questions why
It's rearranged
The past has died
I have no say
To where things lie

So while I face
Tomorrow's smile
I'll show grace
With no denial
The path I trace
May take a while
To find a place
I'm not on trial

Cause I'm not here
If I stay the fool
Drowning in tears
From days so cruel
Rise to greet fear
In each day's duel
For I must adhere
To the game's new rules

REACHING FOR MY GARDEN

Reaching out use to be dismissed
Then it became a necessity
Of self–preservation
A reflex of survival
Past ignorance blinded me to

Now a fixture of my evolution
Planting potential through extending
A branch of vulnerability
Into the light without judgement

The field once fallow
Now finally being tilled
The garden of promise
Full of weeds and wild flowers
All thriving in *my* pasture

▎TENURE

I have tenure to my future
Earning the right to choose
To control
To manifest outcomes
To absorb the whimsy of consequence
Unintended
Yet remain the regent
Of discourse with the Fates
Acquiescing
To my bounded mortality
Where legacy lives through
Adversity

DEFERENCE TO YOU

Pay deference to the moment
With each inhale revere
The cool sweetness of the air
Cleansing 'morrows' fears

Lay defense to the torment
Beseech the shed of tears
To cry in awe of just being there
Sensing wonders drawing near

May common sense now foment
Within reach of longing ears
That you are enough no matter where
Commencing right now, right here

▌ REBIRTH

Christen:
A new beginning
A bon voyage
A welcoming
A rebirth

Depression:
A crumpled hope
A hiatus of joy
A lead shroud
An opportunity for rebirth

Redemption:
A renewed meaning
A salvation
A passionate purpose
An exalted rebirth

▌THERAPY

Therapy
Is being in a decathlon
Never off the grounds
Where the challenges take place
Any rest is fleeting
Before the very best of you
Is required to endure
Once again

How can one be proficient
At everything?
But that is the point
We can't!
We must accept each challenge
Even when mediocrity
Is the expectation and result

Therapy then
Is the learned acceptance
Of the attempt
Where effort wins the podium
Success is the repeating sequence
Of moving one foot in front of the other
To leap the hurdle of challenge
To prove that your heart is willing
Accepting the results
That need not be the Gold
But feel so elated
By the try
An entire life's momentum
Is opened
To endless events

WHY AND THE HOW

Introspection is daunting
It risks reopening
An infected wound
Where inner ugliness
Oozes like blight
Over any potential
Harvest of dreamy aspirations
It does answer the Why, however
It uncovers the deep abscess
Where the lava of self-infliction
Scars the soul when released
Yet, releasing leads to cleansing
Then to healing

This is the beginning of How
And How is not rubbing
An ancient Sumerian tea pot
Manifesting miracles
In a cloud of gold dust
While you render
"It's a whole new world "
With Disney glee
The How is laying sandbag
After sandbag, forging
Your dyke to channel
The fierce current of change
This boundary takes effort, time
And is built only by you

It will also have leaks
Just as clouds loosening tears
To rise over snowy peaks
Natural and inevitable

One is not quarantined
From rogue waves of hardship
Usurping perimeter protections
Flooding the moment's wishful thinking
But not future decades of promise
The How is a work-in-progress
Of rebuilding , innovation and tenacity
It transforms as the Why requires
For Why leads the way to understanding
Ensuring that How's innate ability to do
Is not wasted in
A dreamer's quick fix

DEFINITIONS

Grace . . . is being at peace with the weather of life.
Creativity . . . is imagination with purpose.
Loving another fully is predicated on the sharing and accep-
tance of our vulnerable selves.
Wisdom . . . is deciding to remain a student of the Universe.
Lost . . . is just a confirmation that you're not standing still.
Wonder . . . is the sparkle of impossibility.
Constipation . . . is being full of stored up and wasted oppor-
tunities that bind into a clogged existence going nowhere
Diarrhea . . . is a life moving forward with no substance at all.

TOMORROW'S HAIKU

Tomorrow starts with
Sleep, Wake, then to be Aware
That is a great day!

▌FROM COFFIN TO CRADLE

Convention would proclaim
The title is misguided;
Life has a reversed order

But We who have embraced
The darkness as a comfort blanket
Amidst the turmoil of agony
Beyond limits to sustain
We understand a beginning is waiting
Within the fertile soil of our pain
Our despair
Long asphyxiating our souls
Into a coma of uneasy tranquility

But it is this restlessness
That revives the dormant
Into jolted alertness
Infantile, yet aware
Striving, yet cautious
Wobbly, yet managing
To navigate the precipice
Of Life's cliff
As if some higher self
Becomes compass and harness
Ensuring forward motion

That precarious stance
Against the granite

Is our cradle

From it

A landscape of wonderment beckons

Yet, still the naïve babes

We can barely imagine

Our speechless awe

Once we have reached the summit

▌ I STILL

I still breathe in the essence of him
Like the intoxicating aroma of freshly baked chocolate chip cookies
That lingers long after they have cooled and been put away

I still hear his voice
Like the soothing clickety-clickety chirping of crickets
On a warm, humid summer's night

I still sense his touch
Like calm ocean waves lapping over my feet
And gently tugging on me to follow as they recede

I still feel the awe of him
Like being enveloped by the midnight sky
And the stars which now keep him company

DID AND DIDN'T

I didn't make the bed this morning
Just airing out the sheets
I didn't brush my teeth
Just shielding strangers from my space
I didn't exercise
But I am conserving energy for the exertions of tomorrow
I didn't engage in social media
But neither did any typed word get misinterpreted
I didn't step outside my front door
But I did appreciate the blossoms through the window
I didn't complete my to do list
But neither did the word 'failure'
Enter the vocabulary of the day
I didn't measure up to the productivity of the past
But I did acknowledge
The beauty of me and this moment

THE SCIENCE OF JOY

There is a science to joy
It is the willingness to accept
The test tube of uncertainty
Inserted into the cosmic centrifuge
To deliver a concoction emulsified with whimsy
Where one can choose to splash gleefully in the waves
of randomness
Or be pulled under by the gravity of circumstance
Where the black hole is a theme park or a death spiral

Yet, to be joyous is to be a creator
Still, the Universe has no bias towards creation or destruction
But it is ever expanding nonetheless
In this eternal motion outward
New growth rises from the remnants of collapse
As does hope and renewal
Our bliss becomes an endless stream of questions
Igniting adventures, exploring dreams
Adding substance to our fleeting participation
In the world of 'what if'
For in the dimension of unknown
All of us can thrive
In the continuous voyage of the restless human spirit

THE PONDERING ATHEIST

Is it a prerequisite to 'believe'
Before one is blessed as a 'good' person?
Kindness, respect, compassion do not leave
If we ignore Father, Spirit or Son

If damnation will be my fate perceived
By those who cling to the words of the One
My absence of this grace I shall not grieve
When days in this realm are finally done

No matter the Father's gifts eternal
Blessings abound in rich connection
Free from the anchors of Faith's membership
Where love's freewill escapes hell's inferno
To fully rejoice in each day's perfection
Without daunting fear of sinful slip

▍ PLETHORA

Plethora
Of riches?
Of choice?
Of abundance?
How about a plethora of doubt?!
A menagerie of unanswerables
Acting like a GPS
Assaulted by an immense,
Invisible solar flare
Rendering the world
Directionless
But with inertia yet fueling
Motion into the plasma fog
Of the wandering

There is solace in this
As wandering is not lost
For once one accepts
The pea soup of options
It is not the Unknown that haunts
But the exploration that beckons
The plethora of infinite choice
Becomes the mindset of the Mist Walker
Whose vision fully captures
Landscape's translucent waves
Of possibility

Doubt is now a motivator

Of discovery
As the curiosity
Of a playful soul
Can thrive
Within the infinite haze
Of what's next

TWINKLE IN THE DARK

I have yet to witness my own Starry Night
With swaths of golden gems glimmering
Bursting within the evening's indigo depths
My nights can still sparkle with polite courtesy
As if Van Gogh hit the dimmer switch
On the lustrous hues cast by his brush
But this is enough

For a candle still flickers with only half its flame
A porch is still welcoming with that candle on the sill
My way is illuminated with the soft reassurance
Of understanding midnight and not feeling blind
There is no spotlight to scare monsters
Just me . . . the tiny twinkle in the sky
Who now plays in the dark

THE YOUNIVERSE

This Youniverse is forever expanding
Or retracting
Depending upon the positivity
Or negativity
Of your intentions
It is a colossal source of wonder
And destruction
Like a kaleidoscope of adventure
Amidst chaotic storms

It is a journey traveled
Without a warp-drive
Or di-lithium crystals
The engine is just You
With four sources of fuel:
Ask, Believe, Do and Receive
Ask . . .
What is it that You want?
Believe . . .
Is there a passionate commitment to achieve it?
Do . . .
What actions or resources are needed to make it happen?
Receive . . .
Are you open to the world
Of blessings in your Youniverse?

LOST – PART 3

Looking through a hopeful lens
Observing the adventure in not being found
Suffering only in the failure to try
Trembling in each joyous attempt

IGNORANT ATTITUDE HAIKU

Never mind the pain
Tomorrow will be better
Mind over matter

ALL I ASK HAIKU

I ask for nothing
I ask for everything
A pulse, air and love

STEP TO THE LOVE LIGHT

Lying in the bed I made
Didn't always make the grade
A family hurts in ways that don't fade
Still smile at the door that cracks anew
Arms open wide embracing those dear few
Expressing the love that will always flow through

COLLEAGUES OF COMPASSION

I sit calm and untroubled
In a group of strangers
Brought together through harsh circumstance
Grief, depression, addiction, pain
Bonding us as brothers and sisters
Sharing the deeply engraved
Ashen tattoo of misery on our souls
Like lost sheep bleating the panic
Of relentless wolves in the shadows
There is a collective worry of tomorrow
And the struggle it represents
Always the prey of vulnerability, weakness and doubt
With thriving cortisol presenting its extremes
In the violent vortex
Or vacant vacuum of our Lives

Yet this collective is our strength
Our sanctuary of faces nodding understanding
Or a supportive hand resting briefly on your shoulder . . . no
words needed
Then the awe of witnessing such heaps of courage
To express one's own unique story and pain
Such anguish in this honesty
So raw, so resonating, so real
We are riveted and inspired

By the gift of each other
A gathering of lost souls
Who transform into a single entity
The Colleagues of Compassion

RUNDOWN AND UP BLUES

I had a little crisis as you may know
Depression took me where I shouldn't go
I couldn't rid this darkness inside
It led to attempted suicide

Well Life's vicious swings go to and fro
Didn't want to rise for the daily show
Just curl up in bed, never to rise
I was in for a surprise!

When I was lost I found
Oh! The key to get me off the ground
A brand new reality
And it was staring back at me

The smile in the mirror just seemed to know
Live in the moment and joy will grow
Add a few things to the recipe:
Good friends, good meds and group therapy

There'll be some bumps running down the road
Just roll with it like the river flows
Be proud of the 'try' and you will see
You're thrivin' to full recovery

Hope for tomorrow, like a wind will blow
The breeze of purpose will begin to show
Feel each blessing so happily
That's your new reality

CANDLES AND INCENSE

Candles and Incense
Versus
Tornadoes and Hurricanes
This is a grudge match for the ages!
Buddha vs Darth Vader in a battle
For me
For my salvation!
The eddies of soothing aromas
A force-field to encroaching and relentless
Dread
Yet I know my enemy well
It's close proximity a reminder
To my awareness
To acknowledge the skills of the foe
And its tenacity to destroy
It is time to call in reinforcements
And light 3 more candles

THIS REALITY

I . . .
Does that really mean 'ME'?
Do I actually register
Within this reality
Why? . . .
Does that question not free
The answers to confer
A means for stability
My . . .
Truth is in formation
A big-bang of dust
With no clear delineation
Lie . . .
In this powder of creation
Where blossoms may thrust
Into morning's anticipation
Cry . . .
With awakening anew
Forging through terrain
Appreciating the view
Sigh . . .
With the lens of a different hue
Not darkened with pain
But brightened anew

▌RICHER EXISTENCE

There is a richer existence waiting
As if seeing *small* became big
The bug on the windshield
Becomes organic acrylic paints
Forming the abstract splatter
Of black, green and gold
This has a unique value
Am I becoming a *sommelier* of observation?
Where each second matters
A minute becomes a theme park
A day . . . something to inspire Marco Polo

So what do I sense in this moment?
The laptop keys are slightly sticky
From the remnants of butter chicken
On my fingers
The ice cube just cracked in my glass of water
The soft hum of the fan is an actual note
I hold my breath each time I complete
A thought on this page
I always cross my ankles
Right over left
And I am beginning to grin
As I write this last line

YOU CAN

You feel alive
When another
Is in greater need
Than you
And you act upon that awareness

You feel worthy
When the nay-sayers
Have been shamed
By your efforts
And you do not 'rub it in'

You feel redemption
When the rise of the sun
No longer means
Another day of guilt
And you do not deny this fact

You feel loved
When you have moved beyond
The self-loathing
Of your past
And you can embrace the warmth around you

Scott McBride's struggle with depression, anxiety and grief forced him to acknowledge the illogical, seemingly insurmountable abyss of mental illness, through writing poetry. The poems are raw, visceral illuminations of Despair and Struggle. Rare gems of dark humour are interspersed with self-destruction. These smiles, and even occasional bouts of silliness, create a momentum of hope for eventual Redemption. The author's path to that healing port is a long and precarious one. Yet, by revealing his breathtaking courage and vulnerability. Scott McBride's literary endeavour acts as the sail to whisk him towards this destination.

Scott McBride is a father of 3 and a respected Educator living in Ontario, Canada. The author enjoys painting, sports cars with a manual gearbox, and playing an awesome blues guitar.